Conversations

in Justice

◆

SMALL GROUP
STUDY GUIDE

TIM LATHAM
TRAVIS SIMONE

VIDEO SERIES
DOUG BUNN, TRAVIS SIMONE,
AND RICH SYLVESTER *WITH* TIM LATHAM

A COMPANION RESOURCE TO

GENEROUS JUSTICE
How God's Grace Makes Us Just
TIMOTHY KELLER

To order copies for congregational use, visit:
wcchapel.org/conversationsinjustice

We want to hear from you!
Please send any comments or questions about
this book to: *conversationsinjustice@wcchapel.org*
Thank you.

WILLIAMSBURG
COMMUNITY
⌂ CHAPEL

3899 John Tyler Hwy.
Williamsburg, VA 23185
757-229-7152

wcchapel.org

Conversations in Justice: Small Group Study Guide for *Generous Justice*
Copyright © 2014 by Williamsburg Community Chapel

Scriptures taken from the Holy Bible, New International Version®, NIV®.
Copyright ©1984, by Biblica, Inc.™ Used by permission of Zondervan. All rights
reserved worldwide. www.zondervan.com. The "NIV" and "New International
Version" are trademarks registered in the United States Patent and Trademark
Office by Biblica, Inc.™

This Guide was created as a companion resource for *Generous Justice* by Timothy
Keller. However, it was not created by Timothy Keller or his publishing company.
All quoted words are from *Generous Justice: How God's Grace Makes Us Just*
Copyright ©2010, by Timothy Keller and Penguin Publishing.

INTRODUCTION

Each fall our entire church commits to study the same book of the Bible along with a corollary resource that sheds additional light on that part of scripture and challenges our congregation to grow our faith in an area we may have previously neglected. The following study guide was first used by the Williamsburg Community Chapel in Williamsburg, VA in one of these church-wide studies on the Gospel of Luke and Tim Keller's book, *Generous Justice: How God's Grace Makes Us Just.*

As the fall of 2013 approached, I found myself in the role of Interim Lead Pastor with the need to choose the year's church-wide study topic. The church was in a season of transition and needed to be shepherded with care. However, I knew that in addition to gentle, steady leadership, the church needed to sense that God was not done using our family of faith to accomplish His purposes in the world. In times of transition, churches face the temptation to turn inward when what is needed is a turn outward. A look out instead of in shows us the world for which Jesus died. It pushes us to be awed once again that "God so loved the world..." As I was discerning the best possible study topic for our church, I was confronted by God's great love for the world. It pushed me to ask, does our small expression of Jesus' body called the Williamsburg Community Chapel reflect that love accurately? Answering this question was the key to charting a course forward for us as a congregation.

In order to ask such a question, I knew we needed the right resource to help guide the conversation. Our church had a reputation of strong Bible teaching for over three decades of ministry, yet we had never intentionally studied what the Bible had to say about God's love and compassion for the poor, the fatherless, the alien and the widow. In order to have this conversation productively, I knew we needed a conversation partner that our congregation trusted, one that came from a place of full commitment to the inspiration and authority of God's Word and one that systematically laid out what the Bible has to say about how grace pushes us to serve the least, the last and the lost of our world.

After reviewing several books on the subject of Christian engagement with issues of justice, mercy and compassion, I knew Tim Keller's book, *Generous Justice: How God's Grace Makes Us Just*, was the one that would speak most clearly and convincingly to our congregation. There was one problem; there was no associated small group resource to help the church walk through the content in the context of Christian community. However, because I knew this conversation was exceedingly important to get right, I, along with the other pastors, faithfully assisted by a talented pastoral intern decided to embark on the adventure of creating our own resource for our church.

The following study guide is the result of our work. It is far from perfect. In fact, in the first video session, I talk about how Jesus reaching out to us when we were dead in our sins means we must consider how we are reaching out to those who are dead spiritually and physically (the elders never did approve my request for increased funding for our outreach to the physically dead). The study guide does, however, represent the authentic struggle of one community to engage difficult concepts of scripture in a way that pushed us toward a deeper understanding of God's call to love as He loves. My prayer is that God can use this little resource to help you engage the far more profound work of Timothy Keller in *Generous Justice,* so that your church can engage the most profound work of all, to "let no debt remain outstanding, except the continual debt to love one another" (Romans 13:8).

Travis Simone
Lead Pastor, Williamsburg Community Chapel

HOW TO USE THIS STUDY GUIDE

Welcome to *Conversations in Justice*, our companion resource to *Generous Justice* by Timothy Keller. Each section of the guide contains three elements:

1. Individual pre-group study

2. Small group study

3. Moving toward action

The individual pre-group study will help you read through the book, *Generous Justice*, with a deeper level of precision and allow for time to process the material you are reading. The small group study will begin with a video from the pastoral staff at the Williamsburg Community Chapel. Highlighting major themes and important Scripture from a chapter(s) in the book, these videos encourage groups to engage in discussion on the topics found in the chapter(s). The moving toward action element is made of two components: small group and individual application. The small group application provides a practical step your group can take together to apply the material you are learning in the study. The individual application is a deeper step that can be taken if you want to further integrate the biblical principles you are studying into your daily life.

While it may be ideal to engage all three elements of each section, we also want to encourage you both as individuals and as groups to move at a pace appropriate for where you may be on your spiritual journey.

Our prayer is that your group's time together will not merely increase your understanding of what the Bible has to say about justice, mercy and compassion, but catalyze a shift in your approach to your personal relationships, your community, and the world for which Jesus gave His life to redeem.

To access video content for this series, go to: *wcchapel.org/conversationsinjustice*

WEEK 1: *A Foundation of Justice*
Generous Justice – Chapter 1: What Is Doing Justice?
and Chapter 2: Justice and the Old Testament

INDIVIDUAL PRE-GROUP STUDY

Read pages 3-5, "Justice Is Care for the Vulnerable"

What does "doing justice" mean to you?

What does "loving mercy" look like in your life?

Reflecting on Scripture

> "This is what the LORD Almighty says: 'Administer
> true justice; show mercy and compassion to
> one another. Do not oppress the widow or the
> fatherless, the alien or the poor. In your hearts do
> not think evil of each other.'"
>
> ZECHARIAH 7:9-10

*Keller suggests that God's definition of "doing justice" includes
an understanding that any lack of mercy is wrong. Do you agree?
Why or why not?*

Have you ever witnessed a lack of mercy towards the less fortunate? Describe your experience and how that experience made you feel. Is there a passage of Scripture that speaks to how this situation could have been handled more mercifully?

Read pages 5-6, "Justice Reflects the Character of God"

How does having God introduced as the defender of the vulnerable impact your understanding of God?

Justice, mercy, and compassion reflect God's character. How does this impact your understanding of discipleship?

Read pages 7-9, "Is God on the Side of the Poor?"

Can you think of any tangible ways to share God's "zeal for justice?"

Read pages 10-15, "Justice Is Right Relationships"

How does Keller's description of righteousness challenge you?

What might the word "righteous" look like practically lived out in your life, at work, with family, and in your community?

Read pages 21-23, "Christians and the Civil Law of Moses"

What is one way we can continue to reflect the core of these Old Testament laws, which reflect God's character, in our modern context?

SMALL GROUP STUDY

Video

What is your initial takeaway from the video?

What aspect of the video discussion was most challenging to your faith, your understanding of God, the Bible, or the way you approach your life? Why?

Reflecting on Scripture

> If there is a poor man among your brothers in any of the towns of the land that the LORD your God is giving you, do not be hardhearted or tightfisted toward your poor brother. Rather be openhanded and freely lend him whatever he needs. Be careful not to harbor this wicked thought: "The seventh year, the year for canceling debts, is near," so that you do not show ill will toward your needy brother and give him nothing. He may then appeal to the LORD against you, and you will be found guilty of sin. Give generously to him and do so without a grudging heart; then because of this the LORD your God will bless you in all your work and in everything you put your hand to. There will always be poor people in the land. Therefore, I command you to be openhanded toward your brothers and toward the poor and needy in your land.

DEUTERONOMY 15:7-11

What are the excuses we use today for not helping those in need?

How would God address our excuses?

What are some tangible ways to be more "openhanded toward your brothers?"

Reading *Generous Justice*

Read pages 25-28, "A Community of Justice"

Why do you think we are supposed to work against poverty while God says we will always have the poor?

What are some productive ways you, and the Church, could take part in God's mission to limit debt and poverty in your community?

<u>MOVING TOWARD ACTION</u>

Group

Identify people in your life whom you look upon without mercy. Maybe you have seen these people experiencing injustice and you have made excuses not to help. Write their first name on a sheet of paper, and as a group, pray through the list asking God to continue to move in their lives. Further pray that He would give you wisdom as to how you might practically be in relationship with them.

Individual

This week, perform one random act of kindness. It can be a usual household chore, buying a stranger's meal, etc. The key is that you do this without hope for recognition or reward.

Week 2: *Jesus and Justice*
Generous Justice – Chapter 3: What Did Jesus Say About Justice?

INDIVIDUAL PRE-GROUP STUDY

Read pages 41-43, "But That's the Old Testament"

Have you ever felt in your own life that caring for the impoverished was not a primary focus of the Christian life? Please explain your experience or thought process.

Keller writes, "Christ's salvation is a grace that is undeserved." Write about a time in your own life when you felt undeserving of Christ.

Describe a time in your life when you stopped short of helping another because you saw them as undeserving.

Read pages 43-49, "Jesus and the Vulnerable"

How can you avoid neglecting Christ's teaching in Luke 14?

Think about the tension between doing justice and hurting your career, your social standing, etc. Write down some of your thoughts regarding this tension.

Read pages 49-54, "Jesus and the Prophets"

In this section, Keller discusses the interplay between grace and justice. Have you seen someone transform from experiencing God's grace to engaging in a life of mercy, compassion, and justice?

How can we clean the inside of our hearts to avoid the problem the Pharisees encountered in Luke 11:39-41?

Paraphrasing Matthew 25:31-46, Jesus said that "when you embraced the poor, you embraced me, and when you ignored the poor, you ignored me." What would our lives look like if we lived embracing the meaning of Jesus's teaching in this passage?

Read pages 56-58, "Jesus's New Community"

Think through the similarities between the Old Testament law concerning care for the poor and the New Testament perspective offered by writers Paul and James. Write down some connections you find.

SMALL GROUP STUDY

Video

What was the pastor's main takeaway from this chapter? Why was that aspect of the book so challenging to him?

What was one concept from the video that was new to you? How might you be intentional about remembering and processing this idea during the week?

Reflecting on Scripture

> Then Jesus said to his host, "When you give a luncheon or dinner, do not invite your friends, your brothers or relatives, or your rich neighbors; if you do, they may invite you back and so you will be repaid. But when you give a banquet, invite the poor, the crippled, the lame, the blind, and you will be blessed. Although they cannot repay you, you will be repaid at the resurrection of the righteous."

LUKE 14:12-14

John Ortberg, Senior Pastor of Menlo Park Presbyterian Church, often teaches on Jesus's call to "non-strategic relationships." These are relationships that offer no tangible or emotional benefit to you, but that God nevertheless uses to deepen your understanding of discipleship.

What would it look like to deepen your commitment to non-strategic relationships?

> "Go back and report to John what you hear and see: The blind receive sight, the lame walk, those who have leprosy are cured, the deaf hear, the dead are raised, and the good news is preached to the poor."

MATTHEW 11:4-5

Can you think of other passages of Scripture where Jesus mentions caring for the poor and suffering?

Based on these passages, what level of importance do you think Jesus held for "the least of these?"

Reading *Generous Justice*

Read the first paragraph in "A Whole Cloth" on page 54.

How have you seen this idea of embracing private morality or social justice instead of embracing the "whole cloth" play out in your life, the life of the Church, or in the political arena?

How does your thinking or action need to change in order to embrace the "whole cloth?"

MOVING TOWARD ACTION

Group

Jesus was called many things. "Friend of sinners" was among these names, but for Jesus there was no title of greater honor. Take five minutes of silence and reflect on how those around you would describe you if you were not present. Pick three characteristics or traits that you would like to be used to describe you at your own funeral. Craft an outline for this eulogy, and share with the group.

Discuss ways to become the man or woman that your eulogy describes.

Individual

Make a goal involving a change based on this week's discussion. Craft a short-term, intermediate, and long-range plan regarding how to enact this change in your life.

Week 3: *Justice and Your Neighbor*

Generous Justice – Chapter 4: Justice and Your Neighbor

INDIVIDUAL PRE-GROUP STUDY

Read pages 62-66, "Who Is My Neighbor?"

Can you identify with the expert in the law who questions Jesus? Have you ever sought out this self-salvation in your own life?

Who do you believe constitutes your neighbor?

Read pages 66-68, "The Good Samaritan"

Keller asserts that while not everyone you meet is your brother or sister in Christ, they are all our neighbors whom we must love. How does this statement challenge your thinking?

Read pages 68-75, "Objections to Jesus"

What objections to Jesus' teachings have you voiced in your life?

How can you increase your care and support of your neighbors? What disciplines might be needed or employed to draft and enact these plans?

SMALL GROUP STUDY

Video

Was there something from the video you had a hard time understanding or disagreed with? Share your thoughts with the group and see if the group can help provide some insight.

What did you learn about the parable of the Good Samaritan that you had never considered before?

Reading *Generous Justice*

As a group, read "The Great Samaritan" on page 75.

What feelings or emotions might you experience if you were counting on the aid of someone who owed you punishment instead of grace?

Put yourself in the role of the Samaritan and then in the role of the man suffering. What might you be thinking in the two different roles?

What parallels can you draw between this story and that of Christ?

Reflecting on Scripture

> Therefore, since we have been justified through faith, we have peace with God through our Lord Jesus Christ, through whom we have gained access by faith into this grace in which we now stand. And we rejoice in the hope of the glory of God. Not only so, but we also rejoice in our sufferings, because we know that suffering produces perseverance; perseverance, character; and character, hope. And hope does not disappoint us, because God has poured our his love into our hearts by the Holy Spirit, whom he has been given us. You see, at just the right time, when we were still powerless, Christ died for the ungodly. Very rarely will anyone die for a righteous man, though for a good man someone might possibly dare to die. But God demonstrates his own love for us in this: while we were still sinners, Christ died for us. Since we have now been justified by his blood, how much more shall we be saved from God's wrath through him! For if, when we were God's enemies, we were reconciled to him through the death of his Son, how much more, having been reconciled, shall we be saved through his life!

ROMANS 5:1-10

Can you think of a time in your life where you experienced the transition of suffering to hope?

What does it mean to you that God saved you while you were still a sinner? What are the implications of this statement?

How does understanding God's treatment affect the way we see others who need assistance?

Can you think of any person or group of people that you regard as an enemy but who may actually be your neighbor?

What would change if you treated these enemies as neighbors?

MOVING TOWARD ACTION

Group

Over the centuries, people have always sought to apply the Bible to their own lives, circumstances, and time in history. One famous attempt to contextualize and apply the story of the Good Samaritan is found in the "Cotton Patch Gospel." In this Southern adaptation of the story, the Good Samaritan is an African-American woman. Take turns telling a story of how you could see the Good Samaritan playing out in your life. Be the director of your own dialogue.

Discuss situations in which you could live out Jesus's command to "go and do likewise" this week.

Individual

This week, try to approach an adversary as a neighbor instead of an enemy. As you interact with this person, recall the model of Christ dying for powerless sinners.

Week 4: *Why Should We Do Justice?*

Generous Justice – Chapter 5: Why Should We Do Justice?

INDIVIDUAL PRE-GROUP STUDY

Read pages 79-82, "The Importance of Motivation"

What methods of motivation do you think would effectively propel people towards action for the poor in our world?

Read pages 82-85, "Honoring the Image"

What does C.S. Lewis mean by saying that you've never met a "mere mortal?" How does this change your perspective on people?

How can we, as Keller puts it, "honor the owner's house" as we interact with each other?

Read pages 97-100, "Justification and Justice"

Keller writes, "If you are not just, you've not been truly justified by faith." How does this sit with you?

Read pages 101-104, "A New Attitude toward the Poor"

Has there ever been a time in your life when you had a mindset of being, "middle-class in spirit?"

Why does Keller argue that this type of mindset will lead to a lack of care for the poor and diminished passion for justice?

SMALL GROUP STUDY

Video

What is your initial takeaway from the video?

What aspect of the video discussion was most challenging to your faith, your understanding of God, the Bible, or the way you approach your life? Why?

Reading *Generous Justice*

Read pages 88-92, "Recognizing God's Ownership"

What is one success or area of success that you see as a result of your own industriousness?

Can you trace the roots of this back to a talent, circumstance, or opportunity derived from God?

How does a belief that God owns these talents, abilities, and resources transform the way you steward these gifts?

Reflecting on Scripture

"Yours, O LORD, is the greatness and the power and the glory and the majesty and the splendor, for everything in heaven and earth is yours. Yours, O LORD, is the kingdom; you are exalted as head over all. Wealth and honor come from you; you are the ruler of all things. In your hands are strength and power to exalt and give strength to all. Now, our God, we give you thanks and praise your glorious name.

1 CHRONICLES 29:11-13

Why does David see the Lord as the source of all his wealth and honor?

What difference does it make if we take a stewardship approach to our lives as opposed to an ownership approach?

Circumcise your hearts, therefore, and do not be
stiff-necked any longer. For the Lord your God is God
of gods and Lord of lords, the great God, mighty and
awesome, who shows no partiality and accepts no
bribes. He defends the cause of the fatherless and
the widow, and loves the alien, giving him food and
clothing. And you are to love those who are aliens,
for you yourselves were aliens in Egypt.

DEUTERONOMY 10:16-19

Why could the Israelites be characterized as "stiff-necked?"

*Keller talks about how the Israelites were "poor, racial outsiders,"
and yet were acting callous toward "the poor, racial outsiders in
their own midst." Do we have similar lines of division in our own
lives or in our community?*

How can we avoid becoming "stiff-necked" in our daily lives?

MOVING TOWARD ACTION

> "The logic is clear. If a person has grasped the meaning of God's grace in his heart, he will do justice. If he doesn't live justly, then he may say with his lips that he is grateful for God's grace, but in his heart he is far from him. If he doesn't care about the poor, it reveals that at best he doesn't understand the grace he has experienced, and at worst he has not really encountered the saving mercy of God. Grace should make you just." (pg. 93-94)

Group

Craft a group mission statement for just, compassionate, and merciful living in your community. Discuss how to calibrate this mission statement in your personal interaction with friends, family, and colleagues.

Individual

This week, try to discern a specific gift from God that you possess. Find an opportunity to share this talent or treasure with someone else. Approach with no motive other than helping your neighbor by generously using the gifts God has given you.

Week 5: *How Should We Do Justice?*

Generous Justice – Chapter 6: How Should We Do Justice?

INDIVIDUAL PRE-GROUP STUDY

Read pages 109-112, "Always Thinking of Justice"

What do you think it means to "wear justice?"

Read pages 117-119, "Relocation and Redistribution"

What could John Perkin's concept of relocation look like in your community?

Read pages 119-121, "Racial Reconciliation"

What could John Perkin's concept of Racial Reconciliation look like in your community?

Keller writes about two factors of community development: "inviting outsiders to play a role" and "empowering the poor to take control of their own destiny." What was your reaction to these, and are there any additional strategies you might add?

Read pages 122-125, "Grace and Race"

What are the implications of Keller's depiction of Abraham and us as people who have left our cultures but have not really entered into a different one?

Read pages 133-134, "What about the Rest of Us?"

How can your church enact change even in an affluent area?

Read pages 135-138, "Working with People in Need"

Please reflect on the following interrelated questions:

How much should we help?

Whom should we help?

In what way do we help?

SMALL GROUP STUDY

Video

What was the pastor's main takeaway from this chapter? Why was that aspect of the book so challenging to him?

What was one concept from the video that was new to you? How might you be intentional about remembering and processing this idea during the week?

Reflecting on Scripture

As Jesus approached Jericho, a blind man was sitting by the roadside begging. When he heard the crowd going by, he asked what was happening. They told him, "Jesus of Nazareth is passing by." He called out, "Jesus, Son of David, have mercy on me!" Those who led the way rebuked him and told him to be quiet, but he shouted all the more, "Son of David, have mercy on me!" Jesus stopped and ordered the man to be brought to him. When he came near, Jesus asked him, "What do you want me to do for you?" "Lord, I want to see," he replied. Jesus said to him, "Receive your sight; your faith has healed you." Immediately he received his sight and followed Jesus, praising God. When all the people saw it, they also praised God.

LUKE 18:35-43

What can you learn about Jesus's approach to "doing justice" from this passage?

Jesus entered Jericho and was passing through. A man was there by the name of Zacchaeus; he was a chief tax collector and was wealthy. He wanted to see who Jesus was, but being a short man he could not, because of the crowd. So he ran ahead and climbed a sycamore-fig tree to see him, since Jesus was coming that way. When Jesus reached the spot, he looked up and said to him, "Zacchaeus, come down immediately. I must stay at your house today." So he came down at once and welcomed him gladly. All the people saw this and began to mutter, "He has gone to be the guest of a 'sinner'." But Zacchaeus stood up and said to the Lord, "Look, Lord! Here and now I give half of my possessions to the poor, and if I have cheated anybody out of anything, I will pay back four times the amount." Jesus said to him, "Today salvation has come to this house, because this man, too, is a son of Abraham. For the Son of Man came to seek and to save what was lost."

LUKE 19:1-10

What can you learn about Jesus's approach to "doing justice" from this passage?

How do we apply the principles of these passages from Luke to our lives?

"I put on righteousness as my clothing; justice was my robe and my turban. I was eyes to the blind and feet to the lame. I was a father to the needy; I took up the case of the stranger. I broke the fangs of the wicked and snatched the victims from their teeth."

JOB 29:14-17

What would it mean to "put on righteousness" in our lives?

What are some of the obstacles we might encounter while attempting to wear righteousness in our personal and professional lives?

How might we overcome these obstacles?

Reading *Generous Justice*

Read the first paragraph on page 140.

Does your understanding of the Gospel produce a concern for the poor? Why or why not?

Keller writes that "deeds of justice gain credibility for the preaching of the gospel." Have you ever witnessed someone come to faith in Jesus from the starting point of his or her physical needs being met?

Keller says that evangelism and mercy, justice and compassion "should exist in a symmetrical, inseparable relationship." How can we embrace these two concepts in one cohesive action?

MOVING TOWARD ACTION

"Doing justice, then, requires constant, sustained reflection and circumspection. If you are a Christian, and you refrain from committing adultery or using profanity or missing church, but you don't do the hard work of thinking through how to do justice in every area of life—you are failing to live justly and righteously."
(pg.112)

Group

As a group, refer to the mission statement you crafted last week. In light of this statement and this week's study of how to go about doing justice, share a need that you feel called to meet.

What individuals, groups or organizations are already working to meet these needs?

Is your church attempting to meet these needs?

Not solely through financial contributions, but also by utilizing the gifts and talents you discussed last week, how can you support your church and others?

Individual

This week, select one area of your life that others in the world do not have consistent access to—food, electronics, coffee—and fast for 24 hours. During this time, attempt to place yourself in the shoes of those less fortunate than you and ponder how you would like to be approached by a Christian if you were perpetually in this position. Attempt to delineate between the real needs and felt needs you experience during this 24 hour window.

Week 6: *Peace, Beauty, and Justice*

Generous Justice – Chapter 8: Peace, Beauty, and Justice

INDIVIDUAL STUDY

Read pages 170-172, "The Artwork of God"

What do you think it means that God acted as an architect during creation, without any rival?

Read pages 173-175, "Forms of Shalom"

Can you think of an example of social shalom?

Read pages 177-180, "Justice and Shalom"

How can you "weave" yourself into the "fabric" that Keller is discussing?

Keller says, "The strong must disadvantage themselves for the weak, the majority for the minority, or the community frays and the fabric breaks" (pg. 180). What is your reaction to this?

Read pages 181-184, "Justice and Beauty"

Where and when have you experienced the type of spiritual beauty that would compel someone to live a more just, merciful, or compassionate life?

SMALL GROUP STUDY

Video

What biblical concept from the video challenged your perspective the most?

What was your reaction to the pastor's final thought for each small group?

Reading *Generous Justice*

Read pages 184-189, "God in the Face of the Poor"

What is Keller's main proposition in this section?

What is your initial reaction to this proposition?

Reflecting on Scripture

> A poor man is shunned by all his relatives—how much more do his friends avoid him! Though he pursues them with pleading, they are nowhere to be found.

PROVERBS 19:7

> He who oppresses the poor shows contempt for their Maker, but whoever is kind to the needy honors God.

PROVERBS 14:31

What can we learn from these passages about God's perspective towards the poor?

How should the teaching of God's Word—that serving the poor is connected to serving God—change our approach to serving?

"'For I was hungry and you gave me something to eat, I was thirsty and you gave me something to drink, I was a stranger and you invited me in, I needed clothes and you clothed me, I was sick and you looked after me, I was in prison and you came to visit me.' Then the righteous will answer him, saying, 'Lord, when did we see you hungry and feed you, or thirsty and give you something to drink? When did we see you a stranger and invite you in, or needing clothes and clothe you? When did we see you sick or in prison and go to visit you?' The King will reply, 'I tell you the truth, whatever you did for one of the least of these brothers of mine, you did for me.'"

MATTHEW 25:35-40

Describe a time when you failed to see Jesus in the "least of these?" What lessons have your learned since that experience?

Describe a time when you encountered God through showing compassion, love, mercy, or justice to one of the "least of these." How has that experience shaped your faith?

How can you better carry out God's mission of justice, mercy, and compassion to those in your immediate influence?

MOVING TOWARD ACTION

Group

Discuss how your small group will function differently as a result of this study.

Work together to craft a list of the various opportunities you see to participate in justice, mercy, and compassion. Choose one as a group to get more involved with. Establish some level of support or accountability structure to help improve your community.

Individual

Answer the question: How will I live differently now that I may have more understanding on the subject of justice, mercy, and compassion?

Refer to the people within your immediate influence whom you previously identified. Take first steps this week to begin integrating justice in your normal interactions with these people.

65653269R00026

Made in the USA
Lexington, KY
19 July 2017